AMERICAN PLACES
From Vision to Reality

Colonial Williamsburg

by Meish Goldish

Consultant:
Jennifer Wellock, Architectural Historian
Washington, DC

BEARPORT
PUBLISHING

New York, New York

Credits
Cover, © Matt McClain/Shutterstock; 2–3, © iStockphoto/Ron Kacmarcik; 4T, © The Colonial Williamsburg Foundation; 4B, NYPL/Public domain; 5T, © The Colonial Williamsburg Foundation; 5B, © The Colonial Williamsburg Foundation; 6, tinyurl.com/j7e2ydb/Public domain; 7T, tinyurl.com/z3sfpmk/Public domain; 7B, © North Wind Picture Archives/Alamy; 8T, tinyurl.com/zrvj88k/Public domain; 8B, Internet Archive Book Images/tinyurl.com/zrlvxs6/Public domain; 9T, © The Colonial Williamsburg Foundation; 9B, © Everett Historical/Shutterstock; 10, © The Colonial Williamsburg Foundation; 11, © The Colonial Williamsburg Foundation; 12, © The Colonial Williamsburg Foundation; 13, © The Colonial Williamsburg Foundation; 14, © The Colonial Williamsburg Foundation; 15T, NYPL/Public domain; 15B, © Ritu Manoj Jethani/Shutterstock; 16, © iStockphoto/Imagesbybarbara; 17, Ron Cogswell/tinyurl.com/h4fffyx/CC BY 2.0; 18, © Collection of the Massachusetts Historical Society; 19, © Stephen B. Goodwin/Shutterstock; 20T, © Norfolk Southern Corporation; 20B, © StacieStauffSmith Photos/Shutterstock; 21T, © The Colonial Williamsburg Foundation; 21B, © Stefs13329/Dreamstime; 22T, © n4 PhotoVideo/Shutterstock; 22B, Larry Pieniazek/tinyurl.com/jpm3l72/CC BY-SA 2.5; 23L, © Ritu Jethani/Dreamstime; 23R, Chris Erwin/tinyurl.com/zpot8gb/CC BY 2.0; 24T, © Ritu Manoj Jethani/Shutterstock; 24B, © domonabikeUSA/Alamy; 25, © National Geographic Creative/Alamy; 26, © iStockphoto/Bdphoto; 27T, © The Colonial Williamsburg Foundation; 27B, © The Colonial Williamsburg Foundation; 28–29, © Mapping Specialists, Ltd.; 32, © Stephen B. Goodwin/Shutterstock.

Publisher: Kenn Goin
Editor: Jessica Rudolph
Creative Director: Spencer Brinker
Photo Researcher: Editorial Directions, Inc.

Library of Congress Cataloging-in-Publication Data

Names: Goldish, Meish, author.
Title: Colonial Williamsburg / by Meish Goldish.
Description: New York, New York : Bearport Publishing Company, Inc., 2017. | Series: American places: from vision to reality | Includes bibliographical references and index. | Audience: Age 7–12.
Identifiers: LCCN 2016020324 (print) | LCCN 2016020910 (ebook) | ISBN 9781944102463 (library binding) | ISBN 9781944997106 (ebook)
Subjects: LCSH: Colonial Williamsburg (Williamsburg, Va.)—Juvenile literature. | Williamsburg (Va.)—Juvenile literature. | Historic sites—Virginia—Williamsburg—Juvenile literature.
Classification: LCC F234.W7 G458 2017 (print) | LCC F234.W7 (ebook) | DDC 975.5/4252—dc23
LC record available at https://lccn.loc.gov/201602032

For more information, write to Bearport Publishing Company, Inc., 45 West 21st Street, Suite 3B, New York, New York 10010.
Printed in the United States of America.

10 9 8 7 6 5 4 3 2 1

Contents

Back to the Past

William Goodwin was a dreamer. In 1903, he started to form an incredible idea that would transform a small American town. That year, Goodwin had moved to Williamsburg, Virginia, to work as the **rector** of the Bruton Parish Church. He quickly became fascinated by the town's **colonial** history. Many of Williamsburg's buildings dated back to the 1600s and 1700s. Yet the town's past was disappearing at an alarming rate.

This painting shows Bruton Parish Church in colonial times.

William Goodwin

By the early 1900s, many of Williamsburg's historical buildings had been torn down or were falling apart. Modern gas stations, movie theaters, and telephone poles crammed the streets. Goodwin's dream was to **restore** Williamsburg to its original glory. That way, people could see the important role the town had played in the history of America.

Run-down buildings in Williamsburg, before they were restored

Goodwin wanted Williamsburg to be a living history museum. Visitors would be able to see how people from colonial times lived, dressed, and worked.

A Colonial Capital

In 1699, the **capital** of Virginia was moved from Jamestown to Williamsburg. Virginia was the largest of the American colonies ruled by Great Britain. As the center of the colony's government, Williamsburg was the site of the **Capitol**. Lawmakers gathered in this building to make important decisions for the colony. Another significant building in Williamsburg was the Governor's Palace. This is where the **governor** of Virginia lived.

This is a painting of the Capitol as it looked in the 1700s.

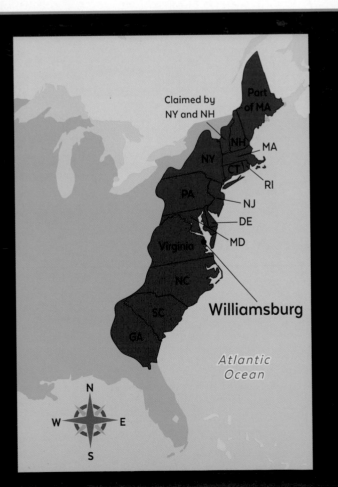

The American colonies

Williamsburg was originally called Middle Plantation. The name was changed to honor King William III of England, who ruled over the American colonies from 1689 to 1702.

The town also had many large churches, beautiful homes, and colorful gardens. In addition, Williamsburg was the center of education in the colonies. The College of William and Mary was one of America's first universities. Its students included Thomas Jefferson and James Monroe, who went on to serve as U.S. presidents in the 1800s.

The College of William and Mary in the 1700s

Thomas Jefferson

Changing Times

In the late 1700s, big changes took place. The American colonies declared their **independence** in 1776, and the United States of America was born. The Americans fought the Revolutionary War (1775–1783) to be free of British rule. In 1780, Thomas Jefferson, Virginia's governor, moved the capital from Williamsburg to Richmond. He feared that Williamsburg, which lay near two rivers, could be easily attacked by British soldiers arriving by boat.

A Revolutionary War battle

Williamsburg was no longer the center of government, and it lost its importance as a major American city. When the first railroads were built in the 1830s, none were constructed in the area. For about 100 years, Williamsburg was just a small, quiet town—until Goodwin moved there.

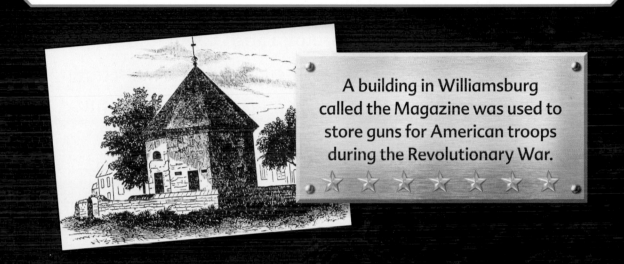

A building in Williamsburg called the Magazine was used to store guns for American troops during the Revolutionary War.

The Magazine, seen here in 1890 after a wall collapsed

Help from a Millionaire

In 1926, Goodwin began his project to transform Williamsburg. He wanted the town to look just as it did in the 1700s, when it was Virginia's capital. He already had some experience taking on big projects. In 1907, he had raised $27,000 to restore the Bruton Parish Church, where he worked. Now he wanted to raise enough money to restore the entire town! However, the huge project would cost millions of dollars. How could he raise that much money?

Bruton Parish Church in the early 1900s, after it was restored to its original colonial look

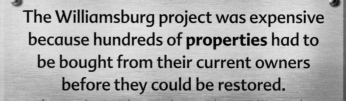

The Williamsburg project was expensive because hundreds of **properties** had to be bought from their current owners before they could be restored.

Goodwin decided to present his bold idea to John D. Rockefeller, Jr., who, at the time, was one of the world's richest people. Goodwin took the millionaire on a tour of Williamsburg and explained his plan with great excitement. He also pointed out that Williamsburg had far more historic buildings than other important towns from the 1700s, such as Boston, Philadelphia, and New York. Rockefeller was very impressed and agreed to provide money for the project.

Goodwin (left) taking Rockefeller on a tour of Williamsburg

Keeping a Secret

Goodwin now had the money he needed, but there was a problem. He feared that some Williamsburg residents might be upset if they knew their town was going to be completely transformed, so he kept the project a secret at first. When he hired **surveyors** to map out the town's buildings and property lines, he had them work under the cover of night.

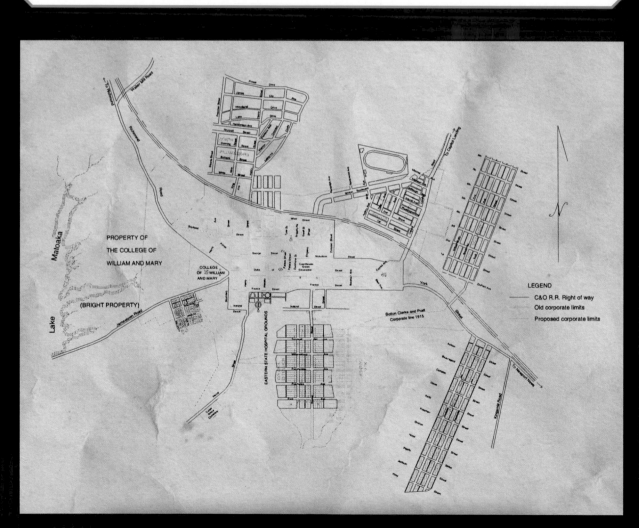

Surveyors made maps like this one to show the location of all the historical buildings that would be restored and rebuilt.

Goodwin also paid for properties without revealing who the real buyer was. Why? He worried that if owners knew the millionaire Rockefeller was involved, they would raise their selling price. When doing business, Rockefeller sent Goodwin **telegrams** in code, such as: "I approve purchase of another **antique**." Rockefeller even signed each message "David's father," using his son's first name instead of his own famous last name to keep his identity hidden.

Williamsburg High School

Townspeople were told about the project in 1928, and few of them objected. When Goodwin announced the news at a meeting in the high school, the crowd cheered.

13

History Detectives

It took a lot of work to plan the living history museum. **Architects** and **historians** had to learn as much as they could about the town's original buildings—but how? Even though there were dozens of historical buildings still standing, many were in terrible shape. Others had been dramatically changed over the years. More than 400 colonial buildings, including the Governor's Palace, no longer stood at all!

Archaeologists found clues about old buildings by digging up parts of the town. They studied **artifacts** that they unearthed from the ground, such as bricks, wooden boards, and kitchen tools.

Archaeologists working at Williamsburg in 1930

Architects wanted to know every detail about each building—its exact color, the kind of roof it had, and the type of stone, brick, or wood that was used to build it. Yet photographs didn't exist in the 1700s. So, architects studied old drawings, paintings, diaries, and maps found in the United States and Europe. This helped them figure out what each building originally looked like.

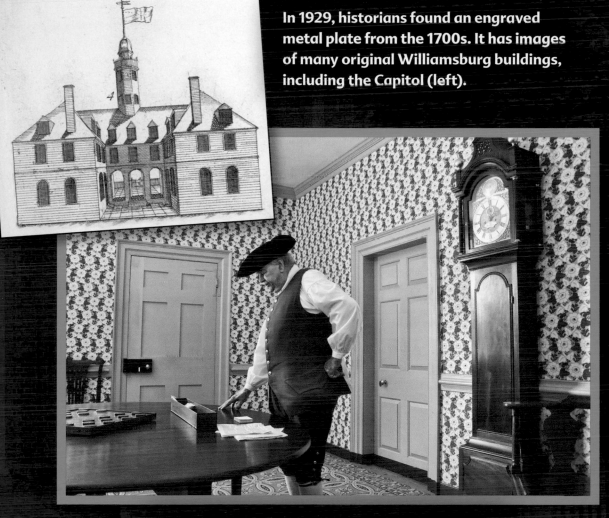

In 1929, historians found an engraved metal plate from the 1700s. It has images of many original Williamsburg buildings, including the Capitol (left).

Researchers learned about the details inside each home, such as furniture, rugs, and wallpaper.

Out With the New

Restoring Williamsburg's old buildings was only one part of Goodwin's plan. The other part was to get rid of all the town's modern features. Anything that was built after the 1700s had to go. As a result, workers **bulldozed** hundreds of buildings. Some modern buildings that weren't torn down were moved to other parts of the town outside the historic area.

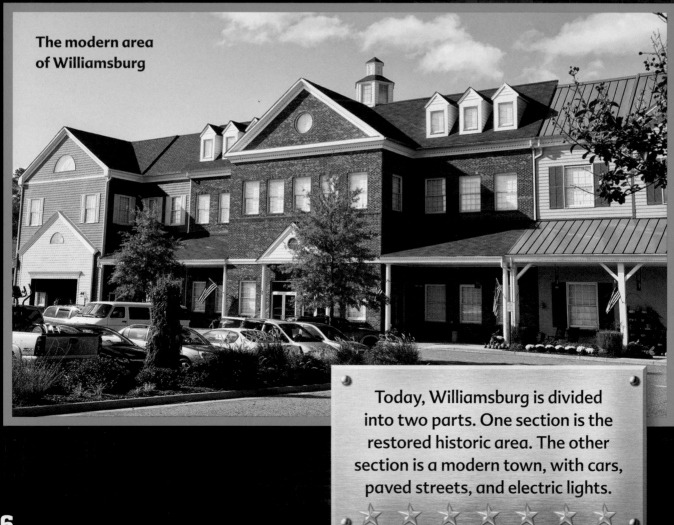

The modern area of Williamsburg

Today, Williamsburg is divided into two parts. One section is the restored historic area. The other section is a modern town, with cars, paved streets, and electric lights.

It wasn't just modern buildings that had to go. On Duke of Gloucester (GLOSS-tur) Street, in the historic area, workers tore up the **concrete** sidewalks and pavement. These were replaced with bricks and sand. Workers also removed the town's telephone poles and electric lights.

Sidewalks in front of the stores on Duke of Gloucester Street are made of brick, not concrete.

Rebuilding the Palace

One of the biggest challenges of the project was the reconstruction of the Governor's Palace. Why? Workers had to tear down the high school and an elementary school so the Palace could be rebuilt on its original location. The Palace had been one of the largest buildings in Williamsburg. Yet historians didn't know much about it. Fortunately, they discovered a diagram of the Palace drawn by Thomas Jefferson in 1779. This helped architects redesign the building's first and second floors.

Thomas Jefferson's diagram of the Governor's Palace

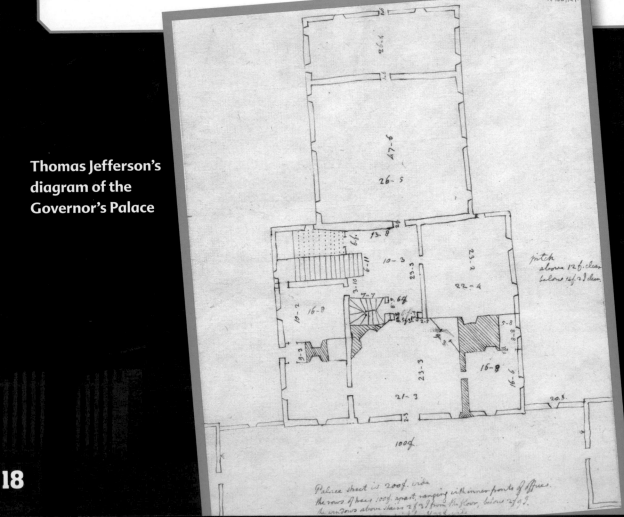

Historians also discovered a document from 1770 that listed more than 16,500 items that had originally been found within the Palace—from furniture and paintings to cooking pots. In addition, a map of Williamsburg from 1782 offered details about the Palace's grounds and **outbuildings**. Finally, after the schools were torn down, archaeologists unearthed pieces of brick that helped workers recreate the Palace's brick walls.

The Governor's Palace, after it was rebuilt

The Palace's main house had burned down in 1781. Some outbuildings, such as servants' rooms and horse stables, survived the fire. However, they were later destroyed during the Civil War (1861–1865).

Then and Now

While some workers completely rebuilt historic structures, others restored buildings that were still standing. That meant removing features added after the 1700s. This was the case for the Courthouse, where trials once took place for accused criminals. In the 1920s, the Courthouse had four **columns** outside the entrance. However, drawings of the building from the 1700s don't show any columns, so workers removed them.

columns

A photo of the Courthouse in the early 1900s

This photo shows the restored Courthouse.

In colonial times, the Ayscough House, located near the Capitol, was just a small home. Years later, the property's new owners expanded the house, making it taller and wider. In 1931, workers on Goodwin's project began restoring the Ayscough House to its smaller size.

A photo of the Ayscough House when it was larger

In this photo of the restored Ayscough House, the building is back to its original size.

In 1930, nail holes and cuts made by saws were found in the wooden frame of the Ayscough House. These clues helped historians to realize the house was once used as a shop. Today it serves as a **gunsmith** shop.

Meet the Colonists

After six years of planning and rebuilding, the living history museum, called Colonial Williamsburg, opened to the public in 1932. Today, visitors can see the restored buildings. They can also meet actors hired to work in the town as colonists. These historical **interpreters** dress and live as townspeople did back in colonial days.

Interpreters act out battles from the Revolutionary War.

Visitors listen as Thomas Jefferson, played by an interpreter, gives a speech.

Interpreters at Colonial Williamsburg learn how to do jobs just as people did them in the 1700s. They make shoes and wigs, build cabinets, and run a **printing press**. Interpreters also sell food and drinks in restaurants called taverns.

An interpreter preparing a meal

A blacksmith crafts a metal item.

Interpreters answer any questions visitors have about what life was like 300 years ago.

Fun for Kids

Visiting Colonial Williamsburg is a special experience for children because they get to enjoy colonial life for themselves. Kids can ride on horse-drawn carriages and get locked in the **stockades**. They can even learn how to make their own candy—and then eat it!

A family rides on a horse-drawn carriage.

In the 1700s, criminals were locked in stockades as punishment.

Many young visitors even share in the same fun activities that kids their age did hundreds of years ago. Modern-day children get to play popular colonial games, such as rolling a large hoop with a stick. They can also make their own toy dolls out of corn **husks**. At Colonial Williamsburg, visitors get to take part in history firsthand!

Children play a game of hoops and sticks near the Governor's Palace.

Keeping the Past Alive

Today, Colonial Williamsburg is still growing and changing. Every year, new **exhibits** are added. For example, some visitors believed the rebuilt town did not do enough to show that slavery existed there in the 1700s. So, in the 1970s, interpreters were hired to **portray** slaves.

An interpreter talks with visitors about what life was like for enslaved people during colonial times.

Colonial Williamsburg is the largest living history museum in the world. It is run by an organization called the Colonial Williamsburg Foundation.

In 2015, historians discovered that the Market House had not been rebuilt correctly. This had once been a place where toys, games, and fresh food were sold. Workers tore down the building and dug up the ground to learn more about the structure's original shape and size. Then, they rebuilt it to look just as it had in the 1700s. Today, Colonial Williamsburg is what Goodwin and Rockefeller had imagined it could be. The town lives up to its **motto**: "That the future may learn from the past."

Shoppers at the Market House

Workers rebuilding the Market House

Colonial Williamsburg

BY THE NUMBERS

Year the Town Was Settled: 1632

Governor's Palace

Everard House

Randolph House

Wythe House

Courthouse

Gunsmith & Foundry

Market House

Magazine

Bruton Parish Church

Duke of Gloucester Street

to College of William & Mary

Number of Years the Town Served as Virginia's Capital: 81

Powell House

Public Jail

Capitol

Raleigh Tavern

Apothecary

Silversmith Milliner

Ayscough House

Cabinetmaker

Shields Tavern

King's Arms Tavern

Wetherburn's Tavern

Tarpley's Store

Mary Stith House

Blacksmith Shop

Glossary

antique (an-TEEK) a very old object that is valuable because it is rare or beautiful

archaeologists (ar-kee-OL-uh-jists) scientists who learn about ancient times by studying things they uncover when they dig in the ground, such as old buildings and tools

architects (AR-kih-tekts) people who design buildings

artifacts (ART-uh-fakts) objects of historical interest made by people

bulldozed (BUL-dohzd) removed from the earth using a large vehicle with a wide blade in front

capital (KAP-uh-tuhl) a city where the government is based

Capitol (KAP-uh-tuhl) the building that serves as the center of government

colonial (kuh-LOH-nee-uhl) during the time when America was a British colony

columns (KOL-uhmz) tall, upright pillars that help support a building

concrete (kon-KREET) a mixture of sand, water, cement, and gravel that is used in construction

exhibits (eg-ZIB-its) displays

governor (GUHV-ur-nur) a leader of a state or colony

gunsmith (GUN-smihth) a person who makes, sells, and repairs guns

historians (his-TORE-ree-uhnz) people who study past events

husks (HUSKS) outer coverings that grow on ears of corn

independence (in-di-PEN-duhnss) freedom

interpreters (in-TUR-preh-turz) people hired by museums to work in costume, preserve knowledge of the past, and share it with visitors

motto (MOT-oh) a saying that states what a person or organization believes in

outbuildings (OUT-bil-dingz) buildings such as barns, outhouses, or shacks that are part of the property where a main building stands

portray (pore-TRAY) to act a part, as in a play or movie

printing press (PRINT-ing PRESS) a big machine that prints books and newspapers by pressing sheets of paper against a surface that has ink on it

properties (PROP-ur-teez) things that are owned, such as buildings and land

rector (REK-tur) a church minister

restore (rih-STORE) to bring something back to its original condition

stockades (stok-AYDZ) devices that lock a person's limbs and head so he or she can't escape

surveyors (sur-VAY-urz) people who measure the position, height, and shape of land

telegrams (TEL-uh-gramz) messages that are sent long distances over electrical wires

Bibliography

The Colonial Williamsburg Foundation: www.history.org/foundation

Greenspan, Anders. *Creating Colonial Williamsburg: The Restoration of Virginia's Eighteenth-Century Capital.* Chapel Hill, NC: University of North Carolina Press (2009).

Kopper, Philip. *Colonial Williamsburg.* New York: Harry N. Abrams (2001).

Stoermer, Taylor. *Colonial Williamsburg: The Official Guide.* Williamsburg, VA: The Colonial Williamsburg Foundation (2014).

Read More

Brenner, Barbara. *If You Lived in Williamsburg in Colonial Days.* New York: Scholastic (2000).

January, Brendan. *Colonial Life (A True Book).* New York: Children's Press (2000).

King, David C. *Colonial Days: Discover the Past with Fun Projects, Games, Activities, and Recipes.* New York: J. Wiley & Sons (1998).

Varela, Barry. *Hogsheads to Blockheads: The Kids' Guide to Colonial Williamsburg's Historic Area.* Williamsburg, VA: The Colonial Williamsburg Foundation (2010).

Learn More Online

To learn more about Colonial Williamsburg, visit:
www.bearportpublishing.com/AmericanPlaces

Index

About the Author

Meish Goldish has written more than
300 books for children. His book *City
Firefighters* won a Teachers' Choice Award
in 2015. He lives in Brooklyn, New York.